One World

What We Wear

Amanda Rayner

W

FRANKLIN WATTS
LONDON • SYDNEY

**Note
about the series**
One World is designed
to encourage young
readers to find out more
about people and places
in the wider world. The
photographs have been
carefully selected to
stimulate discussion
and comparison.

First published in 2004 by Franklin Watts
96 Leonard Street, London EC2A 4XD

Franklin Watts Australia
45-51 Huntley Street, Alexandria, NSW 2015

© Franklin Watts 2004

Editor: Caryn Jenner
Designer: Louise Best
Art director: Jonathan Hair
Maps: Ian Thompson
Reading consultant: Hilary Minns, Institute of Education, Warwick University

Acknowledgements: Jeff Albertson/Corbis: 15. Adina Tovy Amsel/Eye
Ubiquitous: front cover, 16, 22. Richard Anthony/Holt Studios: 19. Quentin
Bates/Ecoscene: 13. Nigel Cattlin/Holt Studios: 14. Jean-Leo Dugast/Still
Pictures: 17. Sarah Errington/Hutchison: 18. John Farmar/Ecoscene: 11.
Ron Giling/Still Pictures: 25. Angela Hampton/Ecoscene: endpapers, 3, 12.
Bob Krist/Corbis: 21. Michael Macintyre/Hutchison: 20t. Nancy Durrell
McKenna/Hutchison: 26. Michael Sewell/Still Pictures: 9. Ariel Skelley/Corbis:
23. Skjold/Eye Ubiquitous: 8. Paul Thompson/Ecoscene: 24. Onne van der
Wal/Corbis: 10. Claudia Wiens/Still Pictures: 20b.

A CIP catalogue record for this book is available from the British Library

ISBN 0 7496 5440 6

Printed in Malaysia

Contents

All kinds
of clothes

People all over the world wear
clothes. The types of clothes they
wear depend on the **weather**
and what the people are doing.

This is a **map** of all the
countries in the world.
Read this book to find out
about the clothes people
wear in different places
around the world.

This boy is wearing jeans
and a tee-shirt. In this book,
you will see people wearing
many different kinds of clothes.

In cold weather

When it is cold, people cover up with lots of clothes to keep them warm. These children in Germany are wearing thick jackets with hats, scarves and gloves.

This is an Inuit family in Alaska, in the United States. They wear heavy parkas to keep out the cold. The fur hoods keep their heads warm.

In hot weather

When it is hot, people do not need to wear many clothes. This family on the beach in Belize have clothes made of light **cotton**. Their hats give them shade from the sun.

This family in Kenya are keeping cool in loose-fitting clothes made of thin **material**.

Keeping dry

When it rains, people need
clothes to keep them dry.
This girl in Canada is wearing
a **plastic** raincoat and boots.
The rain slides off the plastic.

These fishermen from Ireland
wear waterproof overalls and
jackets to keep them dry
when they are at sea.

Clothes for work

People often have special clothes to work in. This woman is a tea-picker in India. She puts the tea leaves into the fold of her sari.

This rancher is riding in a rodeo in Australia. He wears jeans and special **leather** leg guards to protect himself for the bumpy ride!

Uniforms

Uniforms show that people belong to the same group. These girls in Argentina are wearing their school uniform.

In Thailand, monks dress in orange cotton robes so people will recognize them. A sash at the waist keeps the robe in place.

Traditional clothes

▶ The styles of traditional clothes often stay the same for hundreds of years. This girl from Afghanistan is wearing traditional clothes and jewellery.

These men in Cameroon are
dressed for an important event.
They are wearing the traditional
long robes of their tribe.

Wedding clothes

People usually wear traditional clothes when they get married. This bride and groom from Japan wear special **silk** robes called kimonos.

Many brides wear white wedding dresses. This bride in Egypt also wears a bridal veil on her head.

At Hindu weddings, like this one in Trinidad, the bride wears a red sari. The groom wears white, with a special turban on his head.

Dancing clothes

These girls in Spain are flamenco dancers. As they dance, the layers of ruffles on their dresses move in time with the music.

These girls in Britain are dancing in a ballet. They wear soft ballet shoes on their feet. Their skirts are called tutus.

Hats

People wear hats to protect them from the weather. These farm workers in Indonesia have hats made of **bamboo**. The hats protect their heads from the hot sun.

This mother and baby in Bolivia wear hats to keep their heads warm. Their hats are made of **wool**. The baby's hat has flaps to keep his ears warm, too.

Shoes

People wear many different kinds of shoes. These children in China are wearing sandals that keep their feet cool in hot weather.

Trainers are good to wear for exercise and fun. This runner in Britain wears trainers with **rubber** soles to help her feet grip the track.

All around the world

All around the world, people wear clothes.

The countries that you have read about are shown in pink on this map of the world. Find the country that matches each picture in the book.

Canada

United States

Trinidad

Belize

Bolivia

Argentina

Ireland

Afghanistan

Germany

Britain

Japan

China

Thailand

Spain

Egypt

India

Indonesia

Kenya

Cameroon

Australia

Glossary

bamboo a kind of grass grown in some hot places

cotton cloth made from cotton plants

countries places with their own governments

leather material made from animal skins

map a drawing that shows where places are

material something used to make other things

plastic a man-made material used for many things

rubber strong material that comes from a rubber tree

silk a soft cloth made of threads made by silkworms

weather what it is like outside, such as hot or cold

wool heavy cloth made from the coats of sheep and some other animals

Index